THE ULTIMATE 10

Entertainment

TELEVISION MOMENTS

By Mark Stewart

Gareth Stevens
Publishing

Please visit our web site at www.garethstevens.com.
For a free catalog describing Gareth Stevens Publishing's list of high-quality books, call 1-800-542-2595 (USA) or 1-800-387-3178 (Canada). Gareth Stevens Publishing's fax: 1-877-542-2596

Library of Congress Cataloging-in-Publication Data
Stewart, Mark.
    Television moments / By Mark Stewart.
        p. cm. — (The ultimate 10: entertainment)
    Includes bibliographical references and index.
    ISBN-10: 0-8368-9166-X   ISBN-13: 978-0-8368-9166-9 (lib. bdg.)
    ISBN-10: 1-4339-2214-2   ISBN-13: 978-1-4339-2214-5 (soft cover)
    1. Television programs—United States. I. Title.
    PN1992.3.U5S74 2009
    791.45'750973—dc22   2009008293

This edition first published in 2010 by
Gareth Stevens Publishing
A Weekly Reader® Company
1 Reader's Digest Road
Pleasantville, NY 10570-7000 USA

Copyright © 2010 by Gareth Stevens, Inc.

Executive Managing Editor: Lisa M. Herrington
Senior Designer: Keith Plechaty

Produced by Editorial Directions, Inc.

Art Direction and Page Production: The Design Lab

Picture credits
Key: t = top, c = center, b = bottom, r = right, l = left
Cover, title page: (t) Shutterstock, (c) Shutterstock, (c) NASA, (br) Shutterstock, (br) Steve Granitz/WireImage, (bl) Fox/Photofest; p. 4-5: AP Photo/Lucy Nicholson; p. 7, 8, 9: Images of Lucille Ball appear courtesy of Desilu, too, LLC. Unforgettable Licensing and CBS; p. 11: AP Photo; p. 12: CBS Photo Archive/Getty Images; p. 13: Evening Standard/Getty Images; p. 15: AP Photo; p. 16: (t) James Flores/NFL, (b) Kevin Mazur/WireImage; p. 17: (t) AP Photo/M&M Mars, (b) Pixelman/Dreamstime.com; p. 19: (t) NASA, (b) Carolina K. Smith, MD; p. 20: (t) NASA, (b) NASA; p. 21: NASA; p. 23: AP Photo/Evan Agostini; p. 24: (t) AP Photo/Burnett, (b) ©Reuters/Corbis; p. 25: AP Photo/Frank Franklin II; p. 27: AP Photo/Sony Pictures Television; p. 28: (t) NBCU Photo Bank via AP Images, (b) AP Photo/Sony-Jeopardy; p. 29: Jeopardy Productions via Getty Images; p. 31: Frank Carroll/NBCU Photo Bank via AP Images; p. 32: (t) Jacques M. Chenet/Corbis, (b) Gary Null/NBCU Photo Bank via AP Images; p. 33: Carsey-Werner Co. Courtesy Everett Collection; p. 35: Courtesy of CBS Paramount Network Television; p. 36: Interfoto Pressebildagentur/Alamy; p. 37: (t) Industrial Light & Magic/©Paramount/courtesy Everett Collection, (b) AP Photo/Denis Poroy; p. 39: 20th Century Fox/Photofest; p. 40: Mc Pherson Colin/Corbis Sygma; p. 41: Douglas Kirkland/Corbis; p. 43: AP Photo/Lucy Nicholson; p. 44: (t) Kevin Winter/ImageDirect/Fox, (b) Michael Becker/American Idol/Getty Images for Fox; p. 45: Kevin Winter/ImageDirect; p. 46: (t) AP Photo/Harpo Productions, George Burns, (b) Gregg Segal/Corbis

Printed in the United States of America

1 2 3 4 5 6 7 8 9 14 13 12 11 10 09

TABLE OF CONTENTS

Words in the glossary appear in **bold** type
the first time they are used in the text.

THE ULTIMATE 10 Entertainment

TELEVISION MOMENTS

Welcome to The Ultimate 10! This exciting series highlights the very best from the world of entertainment.

Sit back, put down the remote control, and enter the world of television. Channel surf through time. Relive the classic moments when television made history.

Kelly Clarkson sings in the first *American Idol* finale.

What does it take to make great TV? Who are the creative geniuses in front of—and behind—the cameras? What's the difference between a good show and a great one?

This book tells the stories of 10 "ultimate" television shows. Get to know the stars and the people behind the scenes. Relive some of the funniest and most amazing moments in small-screen history. You may never watch television quite the same way again.

Must-See TV

Here are 10 of the greatest moments in TV history.

 I Love Lucy

 The Beatles on Ed Sullivan

 The Super Bowl

 The Moon Landing

 Sesame Street

 Jeopardy!

 The Cosby Show

 Star Trek

 The Simpsons

 **American Idol**

I Love Lucy
The Candy Wrappers

In the 1950s, Americans dreamed of the "perfect" family. This included a husband who went to work and a wife who took care of the house. Lucy Ricardo tried hard to be the perfect housewife, but something always seemed to go wrong. *I Love Lucy* poked fun at the idea that married life was calm and predictable. In one of the show's most famous episodes, called "Job Switching," Lucy learns a not-so-sweet lesson about the candy business.

CHANNEL SURFING

Program: *I Love Lucy*
Air Date: September 15, 1952
Network: CBS
Stars: Lucille Ball, Desi Arnaz, Vivian Vance, William Frawley

In "Job Switching," Ethel and Lucy go to work at a chocolate factory.

Quality Comedy

The first **season** of *I Love Lucy* began in the fall of 1951. At that time, most TV comedies were filmed with only one or two cameras. They were **broadcast** live. The quality of the picture and the sound was poor. Lucille Ball and Desi Arnaz, the stars of *I Love Lucy*, owned their own TV company. Their show had better quality. They used three or four cameras and filmed each episode like a movie.

The crisp images were matched by the quality of the comedy. *I Love Lucy* had great actors and writers. Lucille Ball was amazing. She would stop at nothing to make the audience laugh. Laugh they did. The show was an instant hit.

> **"I am a real ham. I love an audience."**
> —Actress Lucille Ball

Trading Places

In "Job Switching," Lucy and her friend Ethel argue with their husbands, Ricky and Fred. The men say that wives have it easy staying home all day. The women say they would switch places in a minute. They agree to switch jobs.

Ricky and Fred make a mess of the housework. Lucy and Ethel get a job wrapping chocolates. Their job seems fun and easy at first. Then the candies come faster and faster, and they panic. Lucy's solution to the problem is one of the funniest moments in the history of television. She hides some of the candies in her hat and stuffs many others in her mouth.

Lucy's new job is a mouthful.

FOR THE RECORD

Desi and Lucy started a company called Desilu. Its first TV show was *I Love Lucy*. Over the years, it produced other classic television series:

SHOW	STAR	SEASONS
Our Miss Brooks	Eve Arden	1952–1956
The Untouchables	Robert Stack	1959–1963
Star Trek	William Shatner	1966–1969
Mission: Impossible	Peter Graves	1966–1973

Queen of Comedy

I Love Lucy ran from 1951 to 1957. It was at or near the top of the ratings each year. "Switching Jobs" was one of many great episodes. Another was "Lucy Does the **Tango**." In that episode, Ricky and Lucy dance the tango. Ricky, however, doesn't know that Lucy has filled her blouse with eggs. The end of their dance triggered one of the longest audience laughs in television history.

Lucy and Ricky dance the tango. Things will soon get messy.

Reruns of *I Love Lucy* remain popular today. In the 1950s, no one thought TV viewers would want to see the same episode of a TV show twice. *I Love Lucy* episodes have aired thousands of times. Fans keep coming back for more.

DID YOU KNOW?

Lucille Ball and Desi Arnaz were married in real life. In 1953, their son, Desi Jr., was born. That same year, their characters on the TV show also had a baby. About 44 million viewers tuned in to see the arrival of "Little Ricky." The next night, only 29 million people watched Dwight D. Eisenhower's first speech as America's new president.

#2

The Beatles on Ed Sullivan
Beatlemania Begins

Music and video were made for each other. The first group to discover this was the Beatles. In 1964, the "Fab Four" traveled from England to New York to appear on *The Ed Sullivan Show*. Their music was already a big hit in the United States, but Americans had never seen them before. When Sullivan introduced the Beatles, girls in the audience screamed. The music-video age had begun.

CHANNEL SURFING

Program: *The Ed Sullivan Show*
Air Date: February 9, 1964
Network: CBS
Stars: Ed Sullivan, the Beatles—Paul McCartney, John Lennon, George Harrison, Ringo Starr

The Beatles created a sensation when they appeared on *The Ed Sullivan Show* in 1964.

Star Power

Ed Sullivan knew star power when he saw it. In 1956, a young singer named Elvis Presley had performed on his show. Sullivan's ratings soared. In December 1963, he signed the Beatles to appear on his show three Sundays in a row. The group arrived in New York on February 7, 1964, and was mobbed wherever they went. No British band had ever been welcomed to the United States this way.

Two days later, the Beatles took the stage for their live broadcast. Fewer than 800 people were in the audience. When Sullivan introduced the group, they sounded like 8,000.

> **"Broadway was jammed with people for almost eight blocks. They screamed, yelled, and stopped traffic. It was indescribable."**
>
> —Ed Sullivan, about the crowd outside when the Beatles first appeared on his show

Tears of Joy

The Beatles took the stage at the beginning of the program, just after 8:00 P.M. They played three songs, "All My Loving," "'Til There Was You," and "She Loves You." The cameras switched back and forth from the band to the audience. Many fans were weeping with joy.

The Beatles returned in the second part of the show. First they sang "I Want to Hold Your Hand," the most popular song in the country at the time. Then they sang "I Saw Her Standing There." About 73 million Americans watched on television. It was the largest TV audience ever at that point.

Ed Sullivan chats with George, Paul, Ringo, and John.

FOR THE RECORD

The Beatles' first trip to the United States was brief. But they managed to pack a lot performances into their one-week visit.

DATE	LOCATION	PERFORMANCE
February 9	New York City	*The Ed Sullivan Show* (live)
February 11	Washington, D.C.	8:30 P.M. concert
February 12	New York City	7:45 P.M. concert
February 12	New York City	11:15 P.M. concert
February 16	Miami Beach	*The Ed Sullivan Show* (live)
February 23	New York City	*The Ed Sullivan Show* (taped earlier)

Busy Boys

The Beatles appeared on *The Ed Sullivan Show* again a week later. About 70 million people watched the group perform six songs. The group made a third, taped appearance on *Ed Sullivan*, on February 23. Their *Ed Sullivan* performances marked the beginning of Beatlemania in the United States.

The Beatles followed their triumph on the small screen with their first big screen movie. Nine days after returning to England, they began work on their first film, *A Hard Day's Night*.

The Beatles prepare to leave for the United States from a London airport.

"We had heard that our records were selling well in America, but it wasn't until we stepped off the plane in New York that we truly understood what was going on."
—George Harrison

DID YOU KNOW?

Ed Sullivan had first discovered how young people reacted to the Beatles in 1963. While at a London airport, he found himself surrounded by a mob of people. They were there to welcome the Beatles back from an overseas concert.

The Super Bowl
Super Sunday

For a long time, pro football was thought of as a "second-rate" sport. That changed when television came along. Football and TV were made for each other. During the 1960s, the sport grew quickly. There were two different leagues. When they agreed to join forces, TV's biggest event—the Super Bowl—was born.

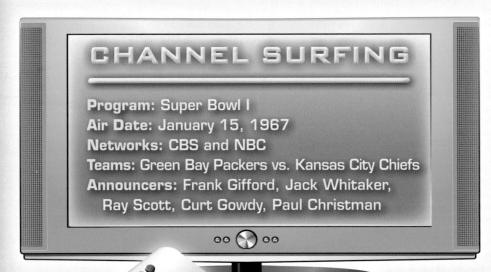

CHANNEL SURFING

Program: Super Bowl I
Air Date: January 15, 1967
Networks: CBS and NBC
Teams: Green Bay Packers vs. Kansas City Chiefs
Announcers: Frank Gifford, Jack Whitaker, Ray Scott, Curt Gowdy, Paul Christman

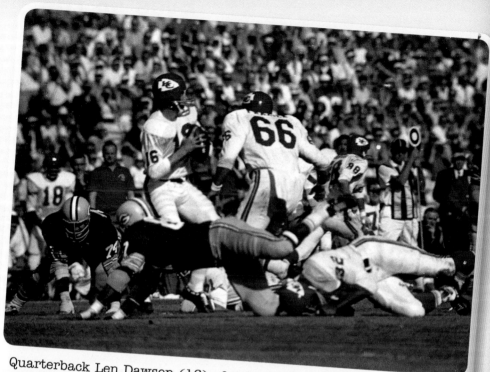

Quarterback Len Dawson (16) of the Kansas City Chiefs drops back to pass in Super Bowl I.

Enough for Everyone

During the 1960s, the National Football League (NFL) and American Football League (AFL) were at "war." Each year they competed to get the best college players. This competition became very expensive. In 1966, the two leagues decided to join to become the NFL. The champions of each league would meet at the end of the season to decide the championship.

In the first Super Bowl, the Green Bay Packers of the NFL played the Kansas City Chiefs of the AFL. NFL games were shown on CBS. AFL games were shown on NBC. Who got to broadcast the first Super Bowl? Both networks aired the game at the same time.

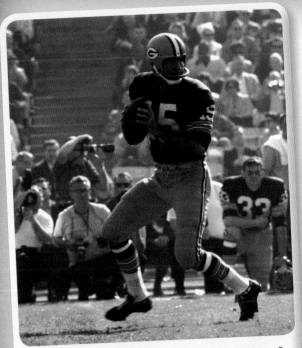
Green Bay's Bart Starr was the star of the first Super Bowl. He threw for two touchdowns.

Eyes on the Screen

Football fans became very excited as game day neared. Even people who did not usually watch football decided to tune in. By kickoff time, almost four of every five TVs in use were tuned to the Super Bowl. The game was close in the first half. In the second half, the Packers ran away with it. The final score was 35–10.

FOR THE RECORD

Halftime at the Super Bowl is almost as fun as the game itself. Besides the great commercials, famous singers entertain the crowd. Here are some of the best:

YEAR	PERFORMER
1993	Michael Jackson
1999	Stevie Wonder
2000	Christina Aguilera
2002	U2
2005	Paul McCartney
2006	The Rolling Stones
2009	Bruce Springsteen

Bruce Springsteen

Halle Berry shares the pool with an M&M character in a 1999 Super Bowl commercial.

Don't Touch That Dial!

More and more people watched the Super Bowl every year. Soon it was the most-watched show on television. During the 1980s, many advertisers started using the Super Bowl to introduce new products. Others aired funny commercials they hoped people would remember.

Advertisers still focus on the Super Bowl. That's because more than 130 million people in the United States watch the game. The cost of a 30-second commercial in the first Super Bowl was $42,000. A 30-second commercial in the 2009 game cost $3 million!

DID YOU KNOW?

The owner of the Kansas City Chiefs wanted a short, catchy title for the AFL-NFL Championship Game. He called it the Super Bowl. He got the idea from his daughter's new toy, called a Super Ball.

#4
The Moon Landing
One Giant Leap
For Mankind

In the 1960s, the United States and Soviet Union were in a "space race" to put the first person on the Moon. On July 16, 1969, U.S. astronauts Neil Armstrong, Edwin "Buzz" Aldrin, and Michael Collins blasted off. Four days later, more than 600 million people crowded around TVs. They wanted to see a person step foot on another world.

CHANNEL SURFING

Program: The *Apollo 11* Moon Landing
Air Date: July 20, 1969
Astronauts: Neil Armstrong, Edwin "Buzz" Aldrin, Michael Collins

Buzz Aldrin walks across the surface of the Moon.

Winning the Space Race

In October 1957, the Soviet Union launched *Sputnik 1*. It was the first artificial satellite in space. The U.S. started its space program in response. The space race between the two countries had begun. In 1961, President John F. Kennedy challenged American scientists to reach the Moon by the end of the 1960s. Less than three weeks earlier, Alan Shepard had made America's first human spaceflight.

In 1968, three U.S. astronauts flew around the Moon and returned to Earth. Until then, most Americans had not been excited about space exploration. Now, Americans were gripped by "Moon fever."

"It's one small step for a man, one giant leap for mankind."
—Neil Armstrong, as he first set foot on the Moon

Touchdown

In July 1969, the *Apollo 11* mission would send U.S. astronauts to the Moon's surface. The *Apollo 11* mission included a command module called *Columbia* and a **lunar** module called *Eagle*. Collins piloted *Columbia* into an orbit around the Moon. Armstrong and Aldrin crawled into the *Eagle* and traveled to the Moon's surface.

The world waited anxiously to hear that the two astronauts had landed safely. Six and a half hours later, Armstrong climbed down a nine-rung ladder. He stepped off and put the first human footprint in the fine, gray dust.

There is no wind on the Moon to blow away the astronaut's footprints.

FOR THE RECORD

The Moon is the only place beyond Earth that humans have visited. Only 12 people have set foot on the Moon—so far.

NAME	MISSION	YEAR
Neil Armstrong	*Apollo 11*	1969
Buzz Aldrin	*Apollo 11*	1969
Pete Conrad	*Apollo 12*	1969
Alan Bean	*Apollo 12*	1969
Alan Shepard	*Apollo 14*	1971
Edgar Mitchell	*Apollo 14*	1971
David Scott	*Apollo 15*	1971
James Irwin	*Apollo 15*	1971
John Young	*Apollo 16*	1972
Charles Duke	*Apollo 16*	1972
Eugene Cernan	*Apollo 17*	1972
Harrison Schmitt	*Apollo 17*	1972

Neil Armstrong, 1969

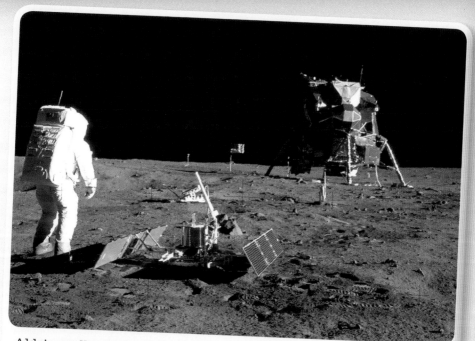

Aldrin walks across the surface of the Moon. People around the world watched the event.

Walkabout

For two and a half hours, the world watched the ghostly black-and-white images of Armstrong and Aldrin. The Moon's gravity is one-sixth of that on Earth. Even with their heavy spacesuits and equipment, the astronauts felt light enough to move around easily. They snapped photos and completed several experiments.

Armstrong and Aldrin planted an American flag, but they did not claim the Moon for the United States. America had "won" the space race. Still, the Moon, said the U.S. government, belonged to everyone.

DID YOU KNOW?

In 2009, a national poll ranked the first Moon landing the most memorable television moment. Barack Obama's presidential victory ranked second.

#5

Sesame Street
Big Bird Sings the Alphabet

Big Bird is one of TV's most lovable characters. He tries hard to learn new things, but sometimes he gets confused. Big Bird makes kids feel okay when they don't understand something. In a 1970 *Sesame Street* episode, Big Bird tries to read a word spelled *abcdefghijklmnopqrstuvwxyz*. As often happens on the show, a simple reading lesson turns into a funny, catchy song.

CHANNEL SURFING

Program: *Sesame Street*
Air Date: Season One, 1970
Network: PBS
Stars: Caroll Spinney as Big Bird

Sign Reader

Sesame Street first aired in 1969. It quickly became popular with both children and parents. The show uses kindness and humor to help kids get ready for school.

Big Bird loves to read. In one early show, he reads all of the signs. He can make out words like *sale* and *closed*. There is only one he can't figure out. It is a sign with all the letters of the alphabet. Big Bird thinks it is one word. He stops his friend Susan and brings her to the sign. He says, "abcdefghijklmnopqrstuvwxyz… it's the most remarkable word I've ever seen." Susan explains that it's the entire alphabet and shows him how to use letters to spell words.

Big Bird, with Elmo, dresses up for a special night.

"If I ever find out just what this word can mean, I'll be the smartest bird the world has ever seen."
—Big Bird, lyrics to "ABC-DEF-GHI"

Jim Henson poses with a crowd of his Muppets characters.

The Muppets

Puppeteer Jim Henson created the original Muppets characters. Big Bird is one of many unforgettable *Sesame Street* characters. Each helped preschoolers learn in a different way. Kermit, Cookie Monster, Grover, Bert, Ernie, and Oscar the Grouch joined Big Bird on the show's first season. Other Muppets, such as Elmo, Zoe, and the Count, were added to the cast later.

FOR THE RECORD

Today, 18 countries have their own version of *Sesame Street*. Here are some of Big Bird's cousins:

CHARACTER	SHOW	COUNTRY
Abelardo	*Plaza Sésamo*	Mexico
Da Niao	*Zhima Jie*	China
Garibaldo	*Vila Sésamo*	Brazil
Pino	*Sesamstraat*	Netherlands

Characters from South African *Sesame Street* say hello.

Sheryl Crow is one of the many celebrities to appear on *Sesame Street*.

Seeing Stars

Sesame Street was one of the first educational programs to invite celebrities to teach kids. Many artists, entertainers, and athletes have been on the show. They include poet Maya Angelou, soccer player David Beckham, actor Denzel Washington, and tennis players Venus and Serena Williams.

Millions of kids around the world have grown up watching *Sesame Street*. The show is clever enough that parents enjoy watching, too. Since *Sesame Street* first aired, many shows have tried to imitate it. None have come close.

DID YOU KNOW?

Big Bird's costume is made of 4,000 turkey feathers dyed yellow. Puppeteer Caroll Spinney has been putting on the huge costume to play Big Bird since 1969.

#6
Jeopardy!
Who Is Ken Jennings?

Game shows have been a part of American life since the 1950s. Winners need a combination of luck, skill, and brains. No game show brought these things together like *Jeopardy!* No player combined these qualities like Ken Jennings. He won 74 shows in a row in 2004, earning a whopping $2.5 million. Jennings proved that *Jeopardy!* was the ultimate game show ... and that he was the ultimate player.

CHANNEL SURFING

Program: *Jeopardy!*
Air Date: November 29, 2004
Network: Syndicated
Host: Alex Trebek
Stars: Ken Jennings, Nancy Zerg

Alex Trebek poses with Ken Jennings to celebrate his 30th appearance on *Jeopardy!* Jennings became the first player to reach $1 million in winnings.

Question-able

Jeopardy! is unlike other quiz shows because it gives **contestants** the answers. Then they must give Alex Trebek, the host, the correct question. For example, the answer might be "The first U.S. president." The first player to correctly ask "Who was George Washington?" adds dollars to his or her score. An incorrect answer subtracts dollars.

Jeopardy! is a difficult game because players must be experts in subjects from rock and roll to outer space. It attracts very smart contestants, and winners return the next show to face two new smart players. The smartest of all was Ken Jennings.

> **"I spent more time with [Ken Jennings] than I did with my wife!"**
> —Alex Trebek, on Ken Jennings's long winning streak

From Art to Alex

Art Fleming was the first host of *Jeopardy!*

Jeopardy! first went on the air in 1964. That was 10 years before Ken Jennings was born. The first host was Art Fleming. He stayed with the show until it went off the air in the late 1970s.

Alex Trebek became the host of *Jeopardy!* when it returned to television in 1984. Until 2003, *Jeopardy!* champions were allowed to play for only five episodes. By June 2004, the longest winning streak was eight games.

FOR THE RECORD

Ken Jennings set many records during his 74-show winning streak:

RECORD	NUMBER
Most *Jeopardy!* prize winnings	$2.5 million
Most *Jeopardy!* appearances in a row	75
Most one-game winnings	$75,000
Highest five-game total	$221,200

Ken Jennings hugs Nancy Zerg after she ended his 74-game winning streak.

The Streak

Jennings's winning streak began on June 2, 2004. As Jennings won more money, more people tuned in to *Jeopardy!* The show's ratings were the highest ever. No one could beat him. Jennings was a trivia expert. He worked in computers, but he knew a lot about subjects ranging from history to hockey.

Jennings lost to Nancy Zerg on November 30, 2004. He was no longer champion. Yet with 74 wins, Jennings had proven himself the best game-show contestant ever.

DID YOU KNOW?

Jennings's winning streak ended when he did not know the answer to a question about the tax-planning company H&R Block. Afterward, the company offered Jennings free tax planning for life!

#7

The Cosby Show
Meet the Huxtables

When Bill Cosby worked as a stand-up comedian, he loved to talk about his family. His comedy routines showed the humor in everyday life. The more Cosby's wife and children drove him crazy, the louder audiences laughed. Could a family television program with Cosby as the father of a large, loving family succeed? In 1984, millions of his fans tuned in to find out. When the first episode was over, America had a new favorite family: the Huxtables.

CHANNEL SURFING

Program: *The Cosby Show*
Air Date: September 20, 1984
Network: NBC
Stars: Bill Cosby, Phylicia Rashad

Kid Stuff

Cliff and Clair Huxtable were more successful than the average American family. Cliff was a doctor, and Clair was a lawyer. They owned a beautiful home in Brooklyn, New York. Never before had a **sitcom** depicted such a successful black family.

The Huxtables' success did not protect them from the struggles of raising a house full of children. They had the same problems as everyone else. The Huxtables had five children. All had different strengths and weaknesses. All had very different personalities. This was one of the things that made the show so real—and so funny.

The Cosby Show ran for eight years.

Cliff and Theo discuss the importance of education.

Cliff & Theo

In his show, Cosby wanted to stress the importance of education. In the first episode, his son, Theo, brings home four D's on his report card. He tells Cliff that a father should love his son no matter how bad his grades are. "That's the dumbest thing I've ever heard in my life!" says Cliff, as the audience roars with laughter. Cliff then uses Monopoly money to show Theo how difficult life will be without an education.

FOR THE RECORD

Popular TV characters often get shows of their own. These shows are called **spin-offs**. In 1987, *The Cosby Show* spun off *A Different World*. It took place in a college attended by Denise Huxtable. Lisa Bonet, who played Denise, left the show after one year. Still, the show was a huge hit. It often trailed only *The Cosby Show* in ratings. *A Different World* ran until 1993.

The cast of *A Different World*

Serious Fun

The Cosby Show used humor to look at serious subjects. Many episodes celebrated the achievements of African Americans. The show rarely talked about racial issues, however.

The warm and funny moments between the Huxtable parents and their children made *The Cosby Show* one of the highest-rated programs in history. It was among TV's top three shows in each of its first six seasons.

Raven-Symoné (left) joined the cast as granddaughter Olivia. She went on to have her own TV show on the Disney Channel.

DID YOU KNOW?

At first, Bill Cosby wanted his character to be a limousine driver who struggled to feed his family. The show's **producers** convinced him it made more sense for both Huxtable parents to have successful careers.

#8

Star Trek
The Trouble With Tribbles

What will the future look like? Will scary aliens rule the universe? Will computers control humans? This is the picture painted by many science-fiction writers. When Gene Roddenberry looked to the future, he saw something else: hope. In *Star Trek*, Roddenberry created a world where humans had solved their planet's problems and were exploring new worlds. Today, Captain Kirk and the crew of the Starship *Enterprise* are still going strong.

CHANNEL SURFING

Program: *Star Trek*
Air Date: December 29, 1967
Network: NBC
Stars: William Shatner, Leonard Nimoy

The crew of the *Enterprise* try to deal with multiplying Tribbles.

Furry Friends

Star Trek often mixed action with humor. The famous episode "The Trouble With Tribbles" is a great example of this. In the episode, the *Enterprise*'s commander, Captain Kirk, and his crew are asked to guard a supply of grain. Soon, their biggest enemies, the Klingons, show up. They want to control the planet where the grain is grown.

> **"Do you know what you get if you feed a Tribble too much? ... [Y]ou get a whole lot of hungry little Tribbles."**
> —Dr. McCoy

Meanwhile, the *Enterprise* crew has discovered cuddly creatures called Tribbles. The more the Tribbles eat, the more babies they have. In no time, the furry creatures get into everything. They drive Kirk crazy. He changes his mind about Tribbles when they help expose the Klingons' plot.

The Future Is Now

Star Trek was a show about the future. Still, almost every plot had something to do with current struggles. *Star Trek* explored issues such as racism, war, and poverty. Many viewers did not realize this until they saw the shows again years later. Roddenberry got this idea from a book called *Gulliver's Travels*. Gulliver traveled the world having wild adventures. Each of Gulliver's adventures also carried an important message.

The *Star Trek* crew proved to be an all-star cast.

FOR THE RECORD

The crew of the *Enterprise* was made up of men and women from different countries. There was also one crew member from another planet!

CREW MEMBER	POSITION	ORIGIN
James T. Kirk	Captain	United States
Mr. Spock	Science officer	Planet Vulcan
Dr. Leonard McCoy	Chief medical officer	United States
Montgomery Scott	Chief engineer	Scotland
Uhura	Chief communications officer	Africa
Hikaru Sulu	Helmsman	Asia

In the 2009 *Star Trek* movie, Zachary Quinto (left) stars as Spock and Chris Pine plays a young Captain Kirk.

New Frontiers

Star Trek fans were heartbroken when the show was canceled after three seasons. Its ratings were low. During the 1970s, *Star Trek* reruns became very popular. The cast was brought back to film a series of 10 movies between 1979 and 2002.

Beginning in 1987, four new TV series went on the air. These shows included different characters and new adventures. In 2009, an 11th movie was released. It showed the original characters when they were much younger.

The original *Star Trek* went off the air more than 40 years ago. Still, it continues to draw new fans and to influence young writers to send their very human characters out into space.

DID YOU KNOW?

Star Trek attracts devoted fans. The most enthusiastic fans are known as Trekkies or Trekkers. They sometimes gather at Star Trek conventions dressed as their favorite characters. At the conventions, they meet actors from the show and buy Star Trek goods.

#9

The Simpsons
Last Exit to Springfield

When *The Simpsons* began airing in 1989, everyone thought it was simply a funny cartoon. Millions of kids had Bart Simpson T-shirts. People quoted Bart. They said things like "Don't have a cow, man" and "Eat my shorts"! Soon fans realized the show had even more going for it. Its lovable characters sometimes seemed more "real" than the flesh-and-blood actors on other shows.

CHANNEL SURFING

Program: *The Simpsons*
Air Date: March 11, 1993
Network: Fox
Writers: Wallace Wolodarsky, Jay Kogen

The Simpsons are a classic American TV family.

Homer Humor

Picking the best *Simpsons* episode is impossible, but many fans and **critics** name "Last Exit to Springfield" as a favorite. The writers filled every frame of this episode with jokes and ideas. The episode has all the weird situations and humor that *The Simpsons* is famous for.

> **"The Simpsons is about ... living with a family who you love but who drive you completely crazy."**
> —Matt Groening, creator of *The Simpsons*

Homer's boss at the nuclear power plant, Mr. Burns, wants to take away the workers' dental insurance. But Homer needs the insurance to pay for daughter Lisa's braces. Homer convinces his fellow workers to go on strike. They win their dental insurance, and Lisa gets her braces!

Culture Shock

"Last Exit to Springfield" makes lots of jokes about books, music, television, and the movies. The title is taken from a book called *Last Exit to Brooklyn*. Lisa's dream looks a lot like the Beatles movie *Yellow Submarine*. There are also jokes about *Batman* and *How the Grinch Stole Christmas*. Reruns of *The Simpsons* are popular. As viewers get older, they like to watch the shows again because they appreciate more and more of the jokes.

The voices behind *The Simpsons* include (left to right) Yeardley Smith, Nancy Cartwright, Hank Azaria, Dan Castellaneta, and Harry Shearer.

FOR THE RECORD

Many of the actors on *The Simpsons* use their voices to play more than one character:

ACTOR	MAIN CHARACTER	OTHER CHARACTERS
Hank Azaria	Moe	Chief Wiggum, Apu
Nancy Cartwright	Bart	Nelson, Ralph Wiggum
Dan Castellaneta	Homer	Krusty, Barney, Mayor Quimby
Julie Kavner	Marge	Patty, Selma
Harry Shearer	Mr. Burns	Smithers, Ned Flanders, Reverend Lovejoy, Lenny, Principal Skinner, Dr. Hibbert
Yeardley Smith	Lisa	

Superstar Series

The Simpsons finished its 20th season in 2009. Its 21st season makes it the longest-running prime-time show in American history. An entire generation has now grown up watching this bizarre family.

Over the years, *The Simpsons* has won more than 20 **Emmy Awards.** With its memorable characters and hilarious moments, the series has taken its rightful place in popular culture. In 2007, the show's success extended beyond the small screen with the release of *The Simpsons Movie.* Their popularity has even earned the Simpsons a star on the Hollywood Walk of Fame.

> **"Homer is so much fun to write for because he's this dumb guy, and the writers take great pride in writing the dumbest jokes for him ever."**
> —Matt Groening

Matt Groening poses with his creations.

DID YOU KNOW?

The Simpsons was created by cartoonist Matt Groening. Groening named the father in the cartoon family after his own father, Homer. Groening's son is also named Homer.

#10
American Idol
It's Kelly!

When *American Idol* went on the air in June 2002, it seemed like just another talent show. Yet by the finals in September, it was a megahit. All eyes were on Justin Guarini and Kelly Clarkson. From thousands of singers who tried out, Justin and Kelly were the last two standing. Fifty million viewers tuned in to see who had won. More than 15 million viewers phoned in their choice. Nothing like this had ever happened on television before.

CHANNEL SURFING

Program: *American Idol: The Search for a Superstar*
Air Date: September 4, 2002
Network: Fox
Stars: Simon Cowell, Paula Abdul, Randy Jackson, Ryan Seacrest, Brian Dunkleman

Born in Britain

Before *American Idol* was created, a show called *Pop Idol* aired on British TV. *Pop Idol* was created by Simon Fuller. Fuller had created and managed the Spice Girls in the 1990s. *Pop Idol* was a talent contest to discover England's best young singer. Fuller asked Simon Cowell, a record producer, to be one of the judges. He was very tough on the contestants.

Fuller hoped an American network would buy the show. At first, everyone turned him down. Luckily for Fuller, Elisabeth Murdoch was a huge fan. Her father, Rupert Murdoch, owned the Fox network. She convinced her dad to buy the show, and *American Idol* was born.

"I knew from the first episode that Kelly was the best one on there."
—Natalie Maines, lead singer of the Dixie Chicks

Kelly Clarkson sings in the 2002 *American Idol* finale show.

Sizzling Summer

During the summer of 2002, *American Idol* became a runaway hit. People loved watching the **auditions**. They featured lots of talented people and some not-so-talented people. The reactions of the judges—Simon Cowell, Paula Abdul, and Randy Jackson—were the best part of the show. They became stars, too!

Besides Kelly Clarkson and Justin Guarini, *American Idol* showcased the talent of Nikki McKibbin, Tamyra Gray, and R. J. Hilton. Season after season, *Idol* would continue to give several great young singers their first chance at fame.

Randy, Paula, and Simon discuss a contestant's performance.

FOR THE RECORD

Over the years, *American Idol* made international stars of these unknown singers:

SINGER	SEASON	FINISH
Kelly Clarkson	One	1
Clay Aiken	Two	2
Fantasia Barrino	Three	1
Jennifer Hudson	Three	7
Carrie Underwood	Four	1
Chris Daughtry	Five	4
Jordin Sparks	Six	1
David Cook	Seven	1

Jordin Sparks

Two for the Money

The winner of *American Idol* would receive a $1 million **recording contract.** The final show aired on September 4, 2002. During the show, Clarkson and Guarini each sang three songs. Two of the songs, including "A Moment Like This," were the same. This way, fans could compare them. Clarkson blew everyone away with her powerful version of "Respect," a hit from the 1960s.

Justin Guarini congratulates Kelly Clarkson on her victory.

When the votes were counted, Clarkson had 58 percent of the vote to Guarini's 42 percent. She was crowned the first American Idol. All three judges agreed with the voters. Kelly Clarkson was a star.

DID YOU KNOW?

After her win, Clarkson released the single "A Moment Like This." It went from number 52 to number 1 on the pop charts in one week—a new record! Whose record did Clarkson beat? The Beatles. As of 2009, she had released four hit albums and won two **Grammy Awards**.

The Oprah Winfrey Show

The Oprah Winfrey Show is the highest-rated talk show in history. Since 1986, Oprah and her guests have discussed important issues. Every weekday, they introduce new ideas to millions of viewers. During a segment called Oprah's Book Club, guests discuss new and classic books. Books often sell a million more copies after being discussed on the show. During one memorable show in 2004, Oprah gave everyone in her audience a new car.

America's Funniest Home Videos

Usually, you have to be in the TV business to get on TV. That changed when *America's Funniest Home Videos* began airing in January 1990. Soon everyone with a video camera had a chance to be a star. The show's producers sometimes receive 2,000 video clips a day. Over the years, thousands of videos have aired on the show, and viewers keep coming back for more. Host Tom Bergeron (left) helps keep everyone laughing.

Glossary

auditions: short performances to test the talent of entertainers

broadcast: sent from a television studio

contestants: people who are trying to win a game or contest

critics: people who write reviews of TV shows, movies, music, and other forms of art

Emmy Awards: award given each year for excellence in the television industry

Grammy Awards: awards given each year for achievement in the recording industry

lunar: having to do with the Moon

producers: people who supervise the making of music recordings, movies, or TV shows

recording contract: an agreement between a singer and a record company in which the singer agrees to make a record and the company agrees to sell it

season: a group of shows played in a row. A television season often starts in the fall of one year and ends in the spring of the next year.

sitcom: a TV comedy about a cast of characters; short for "situation comedy"

spin-offs: new TV shows that arose from previous TV shows

tango: a dramatic dance from Latin America

For More Information

Books

Fisher, Doris. *Kelly Clarkson*. Milwaukee: Gareth Stevens, 2007.

Karol, Michael. *The TV Tid Bits Classic Television Book of Lists*. Bloomington, IN: iUniverse, 2007.

Lasswell, Mark. *Fifty Years of Television*. New York: Crown Publishers, 2002.

Web Sites

The Classic TV Database
http://classic-tv.com
This database of TV shows offers information about classic series.

TV Land
www.tvland.com
Watch episodes and learn more about classic TV shows.

Publisher's note to educators and parents: Our editors have carefully reviewed these web sites to ensure that they are suitable for children. Many web sites change frequently, however, and we cannot guarantee that a site's future contents will continue to meet our high standards of quality and educational value. Be advised that children should be closely supervised whenever they access the Internet.

Index

About the Author

Mark Stewart is the "ultimate" entertainment author. He has written about dozens of television, radio, and movie stars during his career. He also has personal connections to several people in this book, including the cast and creators of *Sesame Street*—whom he worked with for two years. The man who wrote Big Bird's alphabet song was also a family friend. Mark has authored more than 200 books for schools and libraries.